W9-AXK-891

KENNY IRWIN JR.

Jeff Burton

Dale Earnhardt Jr.

Famous Finishes

Famous Tracks

Kenny Irwin Jr.

Jimmie Johnson

The Labonte Brothers

Lowriders

Monster Trucks & Tractors

Motorcycles

Off-Road Racing

Rockcrawling

Tony Stewart

The Unsers

Rusty Wallace

KENNY IRWIN JR.

Ann Graham Gaines

with additional text by **Jeff Gluck**

CHELSEA HOUSE
PUBLISHERS

Cover Photo: Kenny Irwin Jr. won the NASCAR Rookie of the Year award in 1998. His promising career was cut short when he died in a crash during a practice run on July 7, 2000.

CHELSEA HOUSE PUBLISHERS

VP, New Product Development   Sally Cheney
Director of Production   Kim Shinners
Creative Manager   Takeshi Takahashi
Manufacturing Manager   Diann Grasse

Staff for Kenny Irwin Jr.

Editorial Assistant Sarah Sharpless
Production Editor Bonnie Cohen
Photo Editor Pat Holl
Series Design and Layout Hierophant Publishing Services/EON PreMedia

Library of Congress Cataloging-in-Publication Data

Gaines, Ann.
  Kenny Irwin, Jr./Ann Graham Gaines with additional text by Jeff Gluck.
    p. cm.—(Race car legends. Collector's edition)
  Includes bibliographical references and index.
  ISBN 0-7910-8766-2
  1. Irwin, Kenny, 1969—Juvenile literature. 2. Stock car drivers—United States—Biography—Juvenile literature. I. Gluck, Jeff, 1980- II. Title. III. Series.
GV1032.I79G35 2005
796.72'092—dc22

                                                    2005010396

TABLE OF CONTENTS

① A SAD DAY

Tony Stewart had just won $164,000, but there was no reason to celebrate. Rain fell from the sky, and Stewart quietly silenced his race car's roaring engine and drove into the garage without popping a champagne cork or doing a traditional victory lap after winning the New England 300.

It was July 7, 2000. Stewart's mood was similar to that of the 101,000 fans sitting in the steady downpour at New Hampshire International Speedway. Two days after Kenny Irwin Jr. died, no one wanted to celebrate anything.

Stewart and Irwin weren't really friends, but in auto racing, on-track rivals often have a mutual respect for one another even if they do not like each other much.

It was the same for Stewart and Irwin. Both were young, hot-shot drivers trying to make a name for themselves in the National Association for Stock Car Auto Racing (NASCAR). They had raced against each other in lesser-known series before getting to the NASCAR Nextel Cup Series (formerly known as the Winston Cup Series).

In stock car racing, the Cup Series is the major league: before drivers reach the big time, they have to win at the lower, minor league levels.

Race track workers at New Hampshire International Speedway in Loudon, New Hampshire, observe a moment of silence for Kenny Irwin Jr., who died on July 7, 2000, after crashing into the wall during practice for the New England 300.

That is where Stewart and Irwin first began their careers. In smaller cars called "midget" and "sprint" cars, the pair formed a rivalry that continued all the way to NASCAR's top series.

Now, suddenly, Irwin's life had come to a tragic end. While practicing for the New England 300 two days before the race, Irwin's Chevrolet hit the wall of the third turn of the oval track and wrecked.

"We weren't always on the best of terms, but we always brought out the best in each other," Stewart told the media after dedicating his New England 300 victory to Irwin. "We always respected each other."[1]

According to a description of the wreck in *The Washington Post*, Irwin's car hit the wall and then "flipped on its side,

NASCAR officials check the safety wall after a crash at Bristol Motor Speedway in Bristol, Tennessee, during the 2005 racing season. The deaths of drivers Tony Roper, Adam Petty, Kenny Irwin Jr., and Dale Earnhardt Sr. within a ten-month period prompted safety improvements such as "soft walls."

with the driver's side door flush against the pavement, and skidded along the concrete retaining wall. It finally turned over on its roof, and flames shot out from underneath."[2]

The NASCAR community was stunned and deeply saddened. Just eight weeks earlier, another driver, Adam Petty, had been killed after his car hit the same wall on the same track.

It was difficult for the drivers and fans to cope with another death in what was one of the darkest periods in NASCAR history. During a 10-month period, four NASCAR drivers, including Kenny Irwin Jr. and seven-time Cup champion Dale Earnhardt Sr., were killed in racing accidents.

At the time, safety standards were lacking. Today, nearly every NASCAR track has "soft walls," which absorb the impact of most wrecks. Most drivers now use a head and neck restraint system that can save their lives in a violent crash.

Unfortunately, those safety improvements came too late to save Kenny's life so no one will know if they would have been effective.

NASCAR officials concluded that Kenny's throttle probably stuck. The throttle is the part of a car that makes it accelerate. When Kenny was approaching the third turn, he might have not been able to stop his car, NASCAR president Mike Helton told the *The Washington Post*.

"It's a little bit of everything," Helton said about the evidence.

Just eight weeks before Kenny lost his life, Adam Petty (shown above), grandson of the legendary Richard Petty, was killed in an accident at the same turn at the same track where Kenny died.

"The fact that the front brakes locked up and at a point on the track you could still hear the motor revving."[3]

The same thing most likely happened to Adam Petty. The 19-year-old driver represented the fourth generation of NASCAR's most famous family. Lee Petty, Adam's great grandfather, was one of NASCAR's pioneers, and Richard Petty, Adam's grandfather, won the most races in NASCAR history.

Safety equipment just was not good enough. "Adam Petty should be alive today," sports writer Ed Hinton wrote in the *Orlando Sentinel*.[4] "So should Kenny Irwin, another rising NASCAR star who died of nearly identical injuries only eight weeks later. So should five of the six other NASCAR drivers killed in the last decade."

Partly because of the wreck that killed Kenny, NASCAR and its engineers decided to act, striving to make the sport safer for all of its drivers.

DID YOU KNOW?

NASCAR has made many safety improvements since Kenny's death. The most important innovation is called the Steel and Foam Energy Reduction barrier, or SAFER barrier.

The SAFER barrier is a "soft wall," which reduces the impact of a crash by nearly half. The soft wall consists of a material that feels like tough Styrofoam. That foamy layer is bolted onto the concrete wall.

When a car hits the soft barrier, the foam and the bolts flex slightly or bend, absorbing much of the collision's force.

The soft walls have probably saved countless NASCAR drivers from injury since they were installed. NASCAR recommended them for most tracks several years before the mandatory installation date, which occurred in 2005.

THE LONG ROAD TO THE TOP

Kenneth D. Irwin Jr. was born in Indianapolis, Indiana, on August 5, 1969, to Reva and Kenneth D. Irwin Sr. He was the third of their four children, and their only boy. Early in life he started to go by the nickname Kenny. When he became a Cup Series stock car racer, publicists and sportswriters started to refer to him simply as Kenny Irwin, but in his private life he still used the "Jr." in his name.

The Irwin family always loved auto racing. When Kenny was growing up, his family owned a tool rental business, where both his mom and dad worked. After they sold the business in the mid-1990s, however, Kenneth Irwin Sr. fulfilled a lifelong dream and started to build race cars for a living. Kenny's dad and both of his grandfathers had been huge race fans all their lives. While Kenny was growing up, his entire family not only went every year to see the Indianapolis 500, but they also took many trips to see other races. "We never went on a vacation that wasn't to a racetrack," his mother remembered. From the time he was small both he and his dad dreamed that one day Kenny would grow up to race at the Indy 500.

While Kenny Irwin Jr. was growing up in Indianapolis, Indiana, his family always went to the Indianapolis 500 (as shown here in 1994). From his earliest childhood, Kenny and his father shared the dream that someday he would drive in that race.

Kenny "loved anything with wheels from the time he could crawl," recalled Reva Irwin. As soon as he could reach the pedals on a Big Wheel, he always wanted to be outside, riding. She remembers having to watch him all the time because he wanted to go (in her opinion, not his) too far and too fast. When Kenny was 5, his dad and mom bought him a quarter midget racer. Quarter midget race cars are exactly what their name indicates: they are race cars built to look like the popular midget racers teenagers and adults race on dirt or asphalt oval tracks all across the country. Only quarter midgets are exactly one-quarter the size of midgets and are powered by small horsepower Briggs engines or modified Honda motorcycle engines.

The sport started in southern California in the 1930s. Today there are over 3,000 teams of quarter midget racers throughout the United States and Canada. Kids can drive quarter midgets from the time they turn 5 until they are 16 years old. Three national championship events are held each year in late July, early August, and on Labor Day weekend.

Throughout his childhood, Kenny continued to race quarter midgets and then go-karts. As he grew, his dad started to build cars for him. The senior Kenneth also acted as his son's manager and coach. The family went to watch Kenny race practically every weekend. Always strong and a good athlete, he also became a star soccer player while in school. His mother remembers that she always pushed him to develop other interests because she thought that he and his father would get too focused on racing. For example, she also made sure Kenny made time to go watch football games or attend school homecomings.

When he was only 16, Kenny stopped racing go-karts and began racing stock cars. He started his stock-car racing career by competing in races sponsored by the International Motor Sports Association (IMSA). IMSA was then in its heyday. Automobile manufacturers like Porsche, Jaguar, Nissan, and Toyota sponsored teams at IMSA's highest levels. At first Kenny raced stock cars he and his dad worked on.

By the time Kenny graduated from Lawrence North High School in Indianapolis in 1988, he had already been racing for 13 years. He loved to tinker with cars and did so whenever he got a chance. After high school, Kenny went to work in the family's tool rental shop. He always had good business skills, including an ability to work with money, and he got along well with customers. During these years, he also raced cars on a part-time basis. In 1988 he bought his first factory-built race car, a Brick Somerset GTO he raced in IMSA races.

During his five years as a midget racer in the early 1990s, Kenny Irwin Jr. earned a respectable record of 8 wins, 20 second-place finishes, 59 top-5 finishes, and 87 top-10 finishes. A 2004 model of a midget racer is shown here.

In 1991, Kenny became a professional, full-time midget racer. By this time, he was 22 years old and a full-grown man. He had reached his full size, standing 5 feet 11 inches and he weighed about 160 pounds. Driving the car that his family owned and he and his dad had worked on, Kenny took part in the United States Auto Club (USAC) Midget Series. Often he raced against Jeff Gordon, whose stepfather was good friends with Kenneth D. Irwin Sr.

Midgets are specially designed race cars that use full-sized automobile engines. They are what is called an open-wheel car, meaning their wheels are not enclosed in fenders. They have no roofs and they burst with power. Racers take them around short dirt or asphalt courses for just a few miles.

Midget racers start in a novice class and then, as they get more experience, they move through a series of stock classes. Every time Kenny took a small step up in class, he found different opponents and many new challenges. He had to race against better racers with more powerful equipment every time. He got to go faster and faster, which, of course, he loved.

Kenny stayed in professional midget racing for the next five years, through 1996, by which time he was 27. During his years as a midget racer he accumulated a record of 8 wins, 20 second-place finishes, 59 finishes in the top five, and 87 finishes in the top 10. In 1994, he achieved one of his most memorable wins as a midget racer. In his hometown of Indianapolis he beat Mel Kenyon—a long-time midget racer with many victories to his credit—in the Race of Champions at the Mel Kenyon Classic.

In the Midget Series, as in other forms of auto racing, racers accumulate points for every race they run. The better they do in a race, the more points they earn. At the end of the season, the racer who has earned the most points in a series is named champion. In 1996, Irwin won more points than any other midget racer and became the USAC Skoal National Midget Series Champion.

Midget racing has also been the starting point of the careers of other present-day NASCAR stars. Jeff Gordon and Tony Stewart were Midget Series Champions, Gordon in 1990 and Stewart in 1994 and 1995. By the time Irwin earned his championship, he had gotten used to at least a little fame. His victories had been covered by sportswriters in racing magazines. Midget racing fans crowded around to get his autograph.

When he became comfortable driving midget cars, Irwin set himself new goals. He wanted to try to work his way up through the ranks in racing and eventually reach the top. All his life Kenny had worked very hard at racing. After 1993 he not only drove midget cars but also raced sprint cars in the Stoops Freightliner/USAC Sprint Car Series.

Sprint car drivers have a much more grueling schedule than midget racers. There are 70 events every year for sprint cars at 47 tracks in 23 states around the country, so sprint drivers spend a lot of time on the road. In return for their greater time commitment, they get the opportunity to earn more money than midget drivers. Over $9 million is awarded in prize money to sprint drivers every year.

Sprint cars race on short, oval dirt or asphalt tracks, measuring from 3/8- to 5/8-mile in length. Sprint cars are relatively light, weighing only about 1,200 pounds. They feature a tubular frame that completely encloses and protects the driver, who sits on top of the rear axle with his legs straddling a spinning drive shaft. The cars are powered by 410-cubic inch, 800-horsepower V8 engines. Both the blocks and the heads of these highly specialized engines are aluminum, and the valves are made of titanium. The engines do not burn gasoline, but use methanol instead. The two rear tires are huge and floppy, and they differ from each other in size since the cars only turn to the left as they speed around the oval tracks. Sprint cars can go from 60 to 120 miles an hour in four seconds and have a top speed of nearly 160 miles an hour.

Sprint car racing represents a real step up from midget car racing for an aspiring professional racer. Kenny quickly mastered sprint cars. He was the Stoops Freightliner/USAC Sprint Car Series Rookie of the Year in 1993, which meant he had the best record for the season of any rookie. After 1995, he raced a sprint car owned by Gus Hoffman. Altogether,

Irwin won seven races in the sprint series. Just as some NASCAR racers come up from midget racing, others learn their craft in sprint cars. A.J. Foyt, Mario Andretti, Bobby Unser, Al Unser, Parnelli Jones, Billy Vukovich, Tom Sneva, Johnny Rutherford, Gordon Johncock, Gary Bettenhausen, Pancho Carter, and Johnny Parsons comprise part of a long list of NASCAR drivers who once raced sprint cars.

Did you know?

Midget and sprint racing might sound funny, but competing in the USAC-sanctioned series can be a ticket for stardom.

With open-wheel racing series like the Indy Racing League (IRL) turning more toward European drivers, the United States Auto Club (USAC) has become something of a breeding ground for future NASCAR racers.

In recent years, drivers such as Kasey Kahne, Jason Leffler, and J.J. Yeley have made it to the upper levels of NASCAR racing. Kahne was racing well in the USAC series. Two years later, he was the NASCAR Nextel Cup Rookie of the Year, finishing in second place five times.

The American Speed Association (ASA) series has also proved to be a successful training ground for Cup drivers. Jimmie Johnson, Matt Kenseth, Rusty Wallace, and Mark Martin are all ASA alumni.

Once drivers are signed from the USAC or ASA, they typically enter a driver development program for a racing team. Young drivers usually start out at the lower levels of NASCAR racing before moving up.

Kenny Irwin Jr. began driving at age 5 when he got his first quarter midget racer. Although his promising career was cut short, he did spend most of his life doing what he loved best—driving fast.

In 1994, Kenny Irwin Jr. started to race sprint cars in another, more advanced series, called the Silver Crown Champion Series, which is also sponsored by the USAC. The Silver Crown Series is run on a number of courses around the country and attracts the best sprint drivers. Its races have bigger purses than those in the Freightliner Series. In 1994, Irwin made headlines when he won a big Silver Crown race called the Copper World Classic. Over the season he earned enough points to become the USAC Silver Crown Champion Series Rookie of the Year.

Kenny's best race in 1995 was the Tony Bettenhausen Memorial, where for a time he was in last position and then went on to win the race, earning $9,000. He also enjoyed an especially good year in 1996 when he won the USAC Triple Crown and finished second among all racers in points, just missing becoming the champion. His favorite race that year was at the Indianapolis Raceway in his hometown. There he led all 100 laps in the DuPont 100 and beat his long-time idol, Jimmy Sills.

In 1996, Irwin made another big step up. He started to drive in the NASCAR Craftsman Truck Series in addition to USAC events. On September 7, he drove a truck for Jim Herrick in a race at the Richmond International Raceway. He did so well that day—winning the pole in qualifying and coming in fifth overall—that in October Herrick signed Irwin to drive full-time for the Series in 1997. Irwin would drive a truck sponsored by Ford, which was co-owned by Herrick and former basketball all-star Brad Daugherty. When he announced the signing, Herrick said, "This is a great day for Liberty Racing and Ford." Reflecting on the fact that at 27 years old Irwin had already racked up a total of 19 career victories, Herrick continued, asserting: "Kenny Irwin Jr. is one of the top young drivers in the business today."

Established in 1995, NASCAR truck racing is relatively new. However, it has proved a popular attraction. People like to see the powerful race cars that look like pick-up trucks racing at 140 miles an hour. The cars are really the same as those used in NASCAR Nextel Cup or Busch Series racing, except that the engines are a little less powerful.

Kenny's first NASCAR truck race in the new season was on January 19, 1997, in Orlando, Florida. He came in seventh in the Chevy Truck Challenge. In the second race of the season, he did worse, finishing 32nd. The third race was the Florida Dodge Dealers 400, which was held in Homestead,

Racing fans love to watch NASCAR truck racing, which was first introduced in 1995. Kenny Irwin Jr. was named Rookie of the Year in the NASCAR truck series in 1997, beating out 12 other young drivers.

Florida. Irwin started in fifth place. Throughout the race Irwin stayed close to the front, running almost always in the top five. However, five other drivers traded the lead in the first 114 laps. Finally, in lap 115, Kenny Irwin pulled out in front. A lap later, he fell back behind Jack Sprague. Sprague led the race for more laps than any other driver, but a flat tire eventually ruined his chances for a win. In lap 144, the race took a terrible turn when Joe Nemechek crashed his truck into a wall, and tragically sustained a brain injury in the wreck. Nemechek later recovered to continue his career in the Cup Series, but the wreck caused the race officials put out the yellow caution flag, forcing all drivers to slow down while Nemechek's truck was moved from the course. Once they were allowed to get back up to speed, Irwin again took the lead. He led the pack from laps 154 to 162, slipped back for three laps, but then surged ahead for laps 166 and 167—the final two of the race. Irwin won the race over Mike Bliss by a margin of less than a third of a second. His win netted him $44,750 and made him the first rookie to win a NASCAR truck race, he was also the series's youngest winner ever.

Irwin drove in a total of 26 truck races that season. He had some bad days: he finished 28th in Watkins Glen, New York, and 31st in Sonoma, California. However, he also enjoyed another victory at the Pronto Auto Parts 400 in Fort Worth, Texas, in June. His margin of victory was slim at the Fort Worth race, as it was in Homestead: he finished under three-tenths of a second in front of Boris Said. The Fort Worth race differed quite a bit from the Homestead race, however, in terms of speed. In Homestead Irwin had averaged only 98 miles per hour because of the many cautions in that race. At Fort Worth the average speed was 131 miles per hour. Irwin was beginning to reach the speeds he always seemed to thrive on.

Irwin finished his 1997 truck season 10th in the final standings. This was great for a rookie. In fact, he earned enough points during the season to be named the NASCAR Craftsman Truck Series Rookie of the Year for 1997, beating out 12 other drivers. Kenny was quickly showing the big boys in racing that he was one to watch. Throughout his 20 years of racing he kept getting better and more expensive cars to race. His truck races demonstrated that he was ready to move on to another, even higher level.

3

ROBERT YATES SIGNS KENNY IRWIN JR.

The year Kenny Irwin Jr. won Rookie of the Year in the NASCAR truck division, he also made it into stock car racing's big league when he joined the Cup circuit in mid-season. In August 1997, a ceremony was held at the Brickyard in Irwin's home town of Indianapolis celebrating his joining Robert Yates's famous NASCAR racing team. The next year, Yates announced Irwin would take over the seat in Yates's No. 28 Havoline Ford, which had been driven by Ernie Irvan. To get ready for the 1999 racing season, Yates was going to enter a Ford Taurus, No. 27, in a few races with Irwin behind the wheel.

For years Irwin had dreamed of making such a step. His family had always stood behind him, helping him achieve his dreams. In fact, Kenny's family had always been immensely supportive of him in whatever he does. Throughout his career both his parents and his sisters would frequently travel to be with him when he raced. For the ceremony at the Brickyard, Kenny's friends, family, and fans turned out in force. His mother remembers the relief she felt that day, knowing he would get his big break racing stock cars rather than Indy

Kenny Irwin Jr. talks with Robert Yates, who understands Cup Series car engines better than almost anyone else in racing. Yates's teams run near the front of the Cup Series pack year after year.

cars. At the time, she considered stock car racing a much less dangerous sport than open-wheel Indy-car racing. Watching wrecks at Indy she had thought, "This is not good. This is not the right way [for my boy]." She would never forget the week earlier in his career when, racing in a midget race and two sprint races, he had to go to the hospital three times. She believed stock cars would be safer for Kenny to drive.

After Yates's announcement was made, sports writer Curt Cavin, writing for the *Indianapolis Star/News*, called

Irwin "young, adaptable, versatile and marketable." He quoted Robert Yates as saying, "He's our future."

Kenny Irwin had worked hard to get to this position. Ernie Irvan had been driving car No. 28 for Yates. When rumors began to fly that Yates probably would not sign Irvan to a new contract in 1998, Kenny started to make a string of telephone calls to Yates's shop. Libby Gant, Yates's administrative assistant, quickly learned to recognize Kenny's voice. Irwin persisted. Yates apparently was impressed with the phone calls. He said, "If this guy hammers on the guy in front of him like he hammered on my telephone, they'll probably move over."

In joining Yates's team, Irwin had suddenly made it to the top of NASCAR racing. Not only would he be driving in the Cup Series, on the toughest of all NASCAR circuits, but also he would become a member of a very impressive team. Robert Yates's other driver was Dale Jarrett, a veteran racer with many wins to his name. Jarrett won the Daytona 500 in 1993 and 1996. In 1997, he was second among all Cup drivers in terms of points earned. He is expected to keep racing until his tentative retirement in 2007.

Irwin's car, No. 28, was equally impressive. Some stock car fans cheer for a particular driver. Others root for a particular make of car, or the car bearing a particular number. (In reality, stock car owners own several cars labeled with the same number. The cars look identical, decorated exactly alike, but they each run a little differently.) The Cup circuit includes races on short tracks, roads, and superspeedways. One car will be adjusted so that it runs better on the short tracks, for example. Another will be adjusted for superspeedways—perhaps even just one particular superspeedway. Others stand by, ready, in case a car is wrecked.

Kenny Irwin Jr. is seen here driving the No. 28 Havoline Ford, a car with a history of its own. Its previous winning drivers were Davey Allison and Ernie Irvan. When Kenny took Irvan's place behind the wheel, he assumed responsibility for a car worth over one million dollars.

Irwin's No. 28 had been driven for years by the late Davey Allison, who was the victor at Daytona in 1992. Then it was driven by Ernie Irvan, another frequent NASCAR winner. Talking about the car, Kenny Irwin said, "I probably feel more pressure knowing what the 28 car has done in the past. I've been watching it for years. It's got a lot of history."

And his new boss was something of a legend as well. Robert Yates was born in North Carolina on April 19, 1943. At times, Yates has been known as the best engine builder on the circuit. His cars are noted for their phenomenal acceleration out of the corners of race courses. Just as Kenny had to pay his dues to become a driver, so Robert Yates paid his dues as a builder of race car engines. He started at the bottom of a team of legendary stock car engine wizards more than thirty years ago.

In 1968, Yates got a job working on the motors of the Holmon Moody cars. In 1971, he went to work for Junior Johnson, a dominating driver and champion during the '60s and '70s who had also driven for Holmon Moody. In 1972, Yates prepared the motors for Bobby Allison, who was working for and learning from Junior Johnson. The season when Yates worked on the motors was the season that Allison won 10 races and had 24 top-3 finishes.

DID YOU KNOW?

The No. 28 car is not being driven by any NASCAR team as of 2005. Drivers such as Kenny, Ricky Rudd, Ernie Irvan, and Davey Allison had used the No. 28.

The numbers that are used on cars are owned by NASCAR, meaning that the organization can do what it wants with the digits. Teams can request numbers from NASCAR, but the numbers are assigned and are not owned by the individual teams.

No numbers are retired in NASCAR, including the No. 28. The biggest moves to retire numbers were in relation to No. 3 (for the late Dale Earnhardt Sr.) and No. 43 (for all-time victories leader Richard Petty).

It is doubtful any numbers will be retired in the near future.

Team owner Robert Yates, a race car legend in his own right, has been called the best engine builder on the circuit. During his career, Yates built engines for winning drivers such as Darrell Waltrip, Ricky Rudd, and Richard Petty.

Yates moved to the DiGard racing team in 1976, where he worked for 10 years building the motors for such stars as Darrell Waltrip and Ricky Rudd. His cars won over 40 races during that time. Few people realize that it was Yates who provided the engine that Richard Petty used in his 200th career win at Daytona in 1984.

Yates bought the DiGard team from Harry Ranier in 1987, and it became known as the Robert Yates Racing

Thunderbirds. Since 1996, he has been entering two race cars in every Cup race. Today, Robert Yates's cars are known as some of the fastest cars on the circuit, and each year Yates and his team's sponsors spend millions of dollars on them. When Irwin signed on with Yates, he would get some of the biggest sponsors in the game—Texas, Havoline, MAC Tools, Raybestos, and Coca-Cola.

Kenny Irwin had to make some big adjustments when he joined Yates's team. Much more would be expected of him. Cup drivers may only race 36 times annually, but they work far more than 36 days a year. They spend a lot of time in their owners' shops, consulting with their crew chiefs and others about their cars' handling. Every time they race, they spend two or three days at a course, testing a car and qualifying it. They make a lot of public appearances, meeting fans at races, going to press conferences, and talking to sports writers. Throughout the year, they attend functions for their sponsors, meeting corporate executives, for example. So, in joining Yates's team, Irwin would become something of a celebrity. He was assigned a publicist to handle public relations for him. He had to get used to living in the public eye.

He also had to get used to working with a large group of new people. Robert Yates was the owner of Irwin's car and his team manager. But Yates employed more than 80 people to work on Irwin's car. The Ford Tauruses Irwin would take over were very powerful machines. They were all powered by Ford single-cam, pushrod actuated, overhead valve V8 engines, measuring 358 cubic inches. The NASCAR Cup Series race cars that race at Daytona or Talladega may look like the Ford or Chevrolet family car parked in the driveways of your neighborhood, but the only things they have in common are the hood, roof top, and the deck lid. All of the other parts

Kenny Irwin Jr. climbs out of the No. 28 Havoline
Ford after winning the pole position for the 1999
Pepsi Southern 500.

of the car are handmade. Every time he started the igni-
tion on the No. 28 Havoline Ford, Irwin would be assuming
responsibility for a car valued at more than one million dollars, and which had taken more than a dozen people many
weeks to make.

CUP SERIES ROOKIE OF THE YEAR

Kenny Irwin's first Cup race was the Exide NASCAR Select Batteries 400 held at the Richmond International Raceway in September 1997. He drove a Robert Yates Ford Taurus labeled No. 27. To decide the race's starting positions, Cup series events start with qualifying rounds in which drivers start from a standstill at the pit stop. When they pass the finish line their first time around, they reach full speed and take two laps just as fast as they can go. The fastest among all the qualifiers gets to start on the pole, or in the first spot. Irwin practically flew during his qualifying round at Richmond. He ran second fastest among all the drivers, which meant he got to start the race in the second position, on what is called the outside pole. It was a great start to a new phase in his career.

The Richmond race proved exciting for Irwin, too. On lap 21, he was running close to the front of the pack when suddenly his car touched Jeff Burton's. Burton spun out. Three drivers right behind him—Ernie Irvan, Mark Martin, and Hut Stricklin—got tangled up trying to avoid hitting Burton. Irwin sped on. Burton finally got turned around, but by this time he had fallen back to 40th place. In lap 86, Irwin

Kenny Irwin Jr. talks on the team radio as he waits for his turn to qualify for the 1999 Pennzoil 400 at the Homestead-Miami Speedway in Homestead, Florida. During the 1998 season, Kenny struggled to communicate well with the crew and mechanics so they could make the right adjustments to the car.

took the lead from Bobby Hamilton and kept it for 12 laps. By lap 116, Burton, the driver Irwin had bumped, was in the lead. Burton led until lap 283 and then regained the lead again when leader Joe Nemechek gave up first to make a pit stop. Toward the end of the race, in lap 361, Irwin's team-mate Dale Jarrett passed Burton. Jarrett held on and won the race. Having started 23rd, Jarrett came from the farthest back among all winners to date in the season. Irwin got what sports writer David Poole called a "solid eighth." He earned $17,825 for two hours and 45 minutes' work.

This race made Irwin the only rookie in modern NASCAR history to start on the front row and lead the pack in his first Cup race. That race ended up as one of Irwin's career highlights.

His second start was the Hanes 500 at Martinsville, Virginia. He started in third place and stayed in the top ten for most of the race, but a broken fuel pump cut him out of the real competition. He finished 37th. He would go on to appear in two more Cup races in 1997. At the same time, he was still racing NASCAR trucks as well. In October, he and Ernie Irvan—whose place Irwin was taking on Yates's team—entered a truck race at California Speedway. By the final lap, the two were battling for third place. Several times, they bumped into each other. Finally, Irwin inched ahead of Irvan and came in third. Even in the cool-down lap, Irwin and Irvan continued to ram each other. In the garage after the race, they angrily shouted at each other. Irvan pushed Irwin. Afterwards Irvan said, "I'm just not really happy about Kenny Irwin."

By the end of the 1997 Cup season, Kenny had proved to be one of the fastest drivers in qualifying for starting positions each week. Everyone on the Robert Yates Team was impressed with the young man and looking forward to 1998.

The Cup series season starts in February of each year. The first race is held at Daytona, Florida, the birthplace of stock car racing and NASCAR. The Daytona 500 is the most famous of all the stock car races. It's challenging, too. The cars go at speeds of over 190 miles an hour around a big 2.5-mile oval that is banked (tilted) over 30 degrees on the turns.

Racing in the first 125-mile qualifying race, Kenny was involved in the first crash of the 1998 Cup season. On lap 33 of the scheduled 50, Kenny brushed the outside wall coming out of turn two. His car shot back toward the infield and struck Todd Bodine's No. 35 car, which was running alongside. Bodine's car then hit Dick Trickle's No. 90. All three drivers ended up unhurt but unhappy. It occurred so fast that Kenny didn't even know what had happened. Interviewed right after his attempt to qualify, he said, "I was having a ball out there until that mishap in Turn 2. I honestly don't know what happened out there. I can't wait to watch the tape myself. I was just trying to stay in line. I was on the outside and the No. 35 car was trying to get in, but I don't know if he affected the air and that's what got me in the fence or what."

Bodine and Trickle were mad at first that they had been forced out of the race by a rookie, but they calmed down. Sometimes drivers are not so understanding when they are hurt by rookie mistakes.

Irwin's poor showing in the qualifying round meant he started the Daytona 500 in 39th position. He raced well enough to move a long way up, and his was the 19th car to cross the finish line, a whole lap behind the winner, Dale Earnhardt Sr.

Daytona would not be the only course where Kenny Irwin experienced frustration in the spring of 1998. He finished 36th at Las Vegas, 39th at Darlington, 43rd at Bristol, 39th in Texas, and 40th at Talladega. The list of poor showings seemed to go on. His car failed to qualify for the Coca-Cola 600 at Charlotte on May 24, marking the first time the No. 28 car failed to qualify for a race since Yates took over ownership of the team. Kenny could not go fast enough. At the end of the season, he would look back on Charlotte as his biggest disappointment.

The week after Charlotte, at the race in Dover, Delaware, Kenny qualified in the ninth spot on the one-mile banked

Kenny Irwin Jr. (No. 28) is pursued by Billy Standridge (No. 47) out of pit row during the 1998 Daytona 500. Kenny started in 39th position and moved up to a 19th-place finish.

oval track traveling at around 150 miles an hour. But once the race started, the car didn't handle well. Irwin's pit crew made small adjustments in tire pressure, suspension, and handling. But nothing would make the car fast or stable. He finished in 33rd place. After Dover, Kenny explained what he was learning, that natural talent at driving alone wasn't enough to guarantee a good showing in a Cup Series race. "We qualified pretty good for our first race here but struggled during the race. We just couldn't get the setup right. It's difficult here because you really don't know what you need until you make a 100-lap run. You have to kind of figure out how to really race the race track."

Here he used "you" to mean the whole team. How to race a track is the joint responsibility of a group of people, including the driver, the pit chief and crew, and the car's mechanics. Irwin was discovering that he couldn't always communicate well with the crew and mechanics about how the car was handling and what he thought was wrong with it. So, they weren't always able to make the required corrections and adjustments. Kenny said, "The driver sitting in the seat helps make the cars better, and the more experience I get, the more I will be able to help. I look to Dale Jarrett when we go to test and he can do that. I say 'Why can't I,' you know? It's just time figuring that stuff out."

Yates echoed Irwin's sentiments. He said, "It certainly helps when the driver understands the physics of these things. We're not allowed to put computers in here when we're testing and practicing. It's so important that the driver can give you good feedback."

Irwin had one more terrible day in his 1998 season. The 27th race of the 1998 Cup series season was held on a tight, small oval track only a little more than a half-mile in length at Martinsville, Virginia. Ernie Irvan was the fastest qualifier, clocking in at 193.6 miles an hour for the race on September 27, 1998. That day, high temperatures proved nearly unbearable. Irwin dropped out of the race after 175 laps because of heat exhaustion. The eventual winner, Ricky Rudd, had similar problems. The cooling system in Rudd's driving suit broke after only five laps of the race and he endured a temperature of 150 degrees for the hundreds of laps that remained. Afterward, Robert Yates talked about Irwin's season. He said, "We're anxious. We're impatient. We're probably a little bit greedy, but we want to win some races and get going here. . . . We want to be racing in the top ten every week."

The 1998 season held some incredibly down moments for Irwin. But it was hardly all like that. Yates's hope that Irwin would win races seemed reasonable. In April, Kenny Irwin finished fifth in a race at Atlanta. He would have done better except that a lug nut had fallen onto the floor and had to be hunted down during a pit stop. He finished ninth in the race in Richmond in June.

During mid-season, Robert Yates sent Kenny to the Bondurant Driving School in Phoenix, Arizona, to practice his skills for twisty, flat road courses like those at Infineon Raceway and Watkins Glen. When he had been racing trucks, Kenny found that he had a lot of trouble with the road courses. He was not used to the many gear changes the twisty tracks demanded. He explained why they sent him to the school, saying, "The main reason I went out there was to get refreshed with the heel-and-toe technique so you can use the clutch more."

That schooling really paid off for Kenny. He finished ninth at the 350-mile Infineon race on June 28. Infineon has a total of 10 left and right turns. Irwin handled them professionally. On September 12, he got his fourth top-ten finish of the year, coming in 10th in the Exide 400, the 25th race in the exhausting season. He went on to finish 11th in two Cup races later that season, almost being considered a leader. He ended the 1998 season on a high note when he qualified fastest in the last race of the season and started on the pole for the first time in his short career.

In 1998, Jeff Gordon won a total of 13 Cup Series races and was named the series champion for the season. It was a tremendous achievement for Gordon and his chief engineer Ray Evernham. By the end of the year, Gordon had made 33 starts, earned a total of 5,328 points, and won $6,175,867. Mark Martin was Gordon's closest competitor. Martin earned 4,964 points in 33 starts, had 22 top-5 finishes, and won

Kenny Irwin Jr. heads to the start-finish line for the green flag in the 1998 NAPA 500 race at the Atlanta Motor Speedway in Hampton, Georgia. He started the race on the pole for the first time, and he was the only rookie to lead a race that season.

$3,279,370. Between the two of them, Gordon and Martin won over half of the Cup series races.

Kenny Irwin finished the 1998 season in 28th position with 2,760 points. He started in 32 races. He had no wins, one top-5 finish, and four top-10 finishes. He won $1,433,567.

His points total automatically made him Rookie of the Year. Sports writers agreed that as far as rookie seasons go, his had been a real winner. He was the only rookie to appear in 32 races and lead a race in 1998. He was the leading rookie at the end of a race 14 times. No other rookie had even a single top-ten finish. At the beginning of the season, sports writers and fans had seen him as being in competition with rookies Kevin LePage, Steve Park, and Jerry Nadeau. But he had beaten all three handily. Irwin took great pride in his trophy.

Winning the Rookie of the Year award ended Kenny Irwin's first season on the Cup circuit on a positive note. But you only get to be a rookie once, and he never got to enjoy a win in 1998. In 1999, he had to set new goals for himself. At the beginning of the new racing year, NASCAR Online, the official NASCAR Internet site, summed up the stock car racing world's opinion of him. "That's not to say Irwin didn't run well," NASCAR Online said about his lack of wins. Looking to the future, it went on,"You can bet he'll climb in '99. . . . Irwin is learning this game and learning pretty quickly. The Raybestos Rookie of the Year is growing into the famous No. 28 Texaco car."

At the end of the 1998 season, Kenny explained his and the team's long-term goals. He reported, "Robert [Yates] and I didn't sit down at the start of the year and say this is what we want to achieve as far as stats. What we want to achieve is bringing me along as a driver, learning these race tracks and helping get the car set up better. That's what the focus was, that and racing with these other drivers and earning their respect."

In 1999, however, Kenny Irwin shifted his focus. He began to think more about his standings. Over the winter break, between the end of the 1998 season and the start of

Jeff Gordon (left), the 1998 Cup series champion, and Kenny Irwin Jr. (center), the 1998 NASCAR Rookie of the Year, have a laugh with John Andretti at a press conference.

1999, Robert Yates made some changes in his racing team. He divided the people who worked on Irwin's and Jarrett's cars into two separate teams. Each team would work in its own garage. This was more expensive, but it made good sense as it gave the two teams the chance to do things as they wanted. Doug Yates, Robert's son, was in charge of Kenny's engines, and Doug Richert became the crew chief of Kenny's team. Richert and Kenny had worked together before in the NASCAR Truck series in 1997. Richert was considered a steadying influence on Kenny, and Yates predicted good things for the new year. "We accomplished our goal winning Rookie of the Year last year, but didn't exceed our goal at all," he said. "We're certainly looking for bigger and better things from Doug, Kenny, and the No. 28 team in 1999."

There is nothing like the first NASCAR race of the season, which is held at Daytona every February. Imagine the baseball season beginning with the World Series. All winter long, NASCAR teams tinker with their cars, experimenting with new engines, tires, and shock absorbers. They try to create the fastest cars in the world while keeping them stable. By Daytona, the teams are anxious to show off their new machines, to test them out in the heat of a race. At superspeedways like Daytona and Talladega, the cars average over 190 miles an hour on a 2.5-mile track with steeply banked turns. This means while the infield side of the track is at ground level, the outside of the track rises as high as a three-story building. What is amazing is that the cars are capable of going much faster than they actually do. NASCAR has ruled that at the superspeedways, the speeds must be regulated. Otherwise, it would be too dangerous for the race teams and the spectators.

To limit the racer's speed at Daytona, a metal plate with four small holes in it, called a restrictor plate, is placed between the carburetor and the intake manifold. This limits how much air and fuel is exploded in the cylinders in each cycle of the engine's revolution. One effect of these restrictor plates is that all of the cars are limited to the same top speed, and they all can get to that speed at about the same rate. Everything that happens during the race is done at close to full speed. During the race, cars break off into packs that are so close together that the air rushing over the first car creates a draft that pulls the others forward. Any car that wants to pass another has to drop out of the chain and survive the sledgehammer blow of the open air and not wreck. That's the tricky part.

At Daytona, in 1999, Kenny started the race in the back at the 41st position. Once the main event started, Kenny immediately made progress. The changes the race team had made

A NASCAR official examines a restrictor plate as the cars go through technical inspection prior to a race. This thin aluminum plate fits between the carburetor and the intake manifold, limiting the amount of air that can enter an engine. Less air equals less horsepower, enabling slower, safer races.

to the car overnight were exactly right. On lap 15, Kenny was in 31st place; on lap 30, he was in 21st place. The 11 fastest cars ran in front in their own pack. This kind of racing takes daring and skill. In sprint racing, where most of the new NASCAR racers come from, the car has so much power that racing often becomes a sequence of sliding, turning, braking, and accelerating. In contrast, in Daytona racing, where everyone has the same incredible power, a winning driver needs to be cool, trusting, and patient, making split-second decisions and executing them calmly while under tremendous pressure.

In the early laps of the 1999 Daytona 500, Bobby Labonte and Jeff Gordon battled for the lead. Kenny ran in a second pack following a few seconds behind the leaders. On lap 40, Kenny was 15th overall. He had passed 26 other cars to be there. It was obvious that Kenny's car was fast enough to win.

Kenny wasn't alone when he failed to win a race during his Rookie of the Year season.

Only 10 out of the 45 top rookies have won a race during their first year. The 2004 NASCAR Nextel Cup series Rookie of the Year, Kasey Kahne, didn't help those numbers at all.

Not only did Kahne finish in second place five times, but he was winning several other races when his car crashed or suffered various other misfortunes.

With a tough, competitive sport like NASCAR, it can be hard for inexperienced rookies to have an impact. In early 2005, one rookie made a name for himself without even winning a race.

Kyle Busch, the younger brother of former Cup winner Kurt Busch, became the youngest driver ever to win the pole position for a NASCAR Cup race. When he pulled off the feat, he was only 19 years old.

Kenny Irwin had the best seat in the house to watch and learn these little tricks from the seasoned professionals. He sat in third place, immediately behind Dale Earnhardt Sr. "Earnhardt was doing everything he could to get by Gordon. If he had had the lane, I would have probably gone with him. . . . I felt like if he went, I could probably end up second and progressively move up. That's what I did for the last 10 laps. Just try to make the right moves just to keep inching up for the end of the race."

Kenny and the crew were happy to get third. Sports writer Bill Frederickson expressed his surprise at how well Irwin had done there. "Kenny Irwin, who piloted his No. 28 Texaco/Havoline Ford to the third-place position, wasn't supposed to be there," Frederickson wrote in an article he submitted to NASCAR Online. "After all," he went on, "Irwin was running only his second Daytona 500. He was starting just his 37th career series event. And he used a provisional to make the field, at that."

Irwin gloried in his best run ever. He came away from Daytona with his belief in himself confirmed.

We felt like we had a very good race in our Gatorade 125 (the qualifying race), and we finished 16th. We came back, and we said what do we need to do? We made very minor changes, really, to the car. I think that (the third place finish) does a lot for our team. Our team has gone through a lot over the winter, and it's going to help make everybody and myself more confident going into the whole year. We've just got to get more consistent and get a lot more top threes.

Kenny and the crew won $465,084 for the race and 165 points toward the year-end championship. Kenny had done much better than anyone had expected, with the possible exception of himself.

5

KENNY'S LEGACY

The 1999 Daytona 500 was the high point of Kenny's career. There he showed so much promise and potential. Sadly, that was ultimately cut short.

The rest of the 1999 season was not as successful for Kenny. He had one other top-5 finish that year and five other top-10s. That left Kenny in 19th place, and the pressure grew on the young driver.

After reviewing Kenny's performance during his two years with the team, Robert Yates decided to go in a different direction. He released Kenny in favor of veteran driver Ricky Rudd.

It didn't take Kenny long to hook up with a new team, however. The co-owned team of Felix Sabates and Chip Ganassi signed Kenny to drive for them in the 2000 Cup series season. He moved from the No. 28 car to the No. 42 car, sponsored by BellSouth.

Kenny finished fourth at the Talladega race in the spring, but that was his only top-10 finish in 17 starts with his new team. Then came the tragic day on July 7, 2000. During a Cup practice run, Kenny slammed into the wall, likely due to a stuck throttle. Eyewitnesses saw his brakes lock up, but the car wasn't slowing down.

Kenny Irwin Jr. (No. 42) leads the pack during the 2000 Food City 500 race at Bristol Motor Speedway in Bristol, Tennessee. Kenny had 17 starts with his new team before the tragic events of July 7, 2000.

Kenny never got the chance to prove that he was the talented driver that finished third at Daytona and fourth at Talladega in the previous season.

"Irwin never tasted the Cup success that was predicted for him, but he was only 30 years old, so we will never know whether he could have turned his career around," wrote Ryan Smithson on CNN/SI.com.[5] "Considering his abundance of talent, it is probable that he would have."

Rescue personnel carry Kenny Irwin Jr. to a waiting ambulance at the New Hampshire International Speedway in Loudon, New Hampshire. It was the second fatal crash in as many months, prompting investigations and critics to call for NASCAR to suspend racing.

Today, the safety standards in NASCAR have come a long way. In fact, throughout the entire 2004 Nextel Cup season, no drivers were injured on the track. That doesn't mean racing at 200 miles per hour is safe or that it is impossible to be injured or killed on the track. Because of Kenny, there was some good that came into racing's future.

Kenny's family wanted to make sure his life wouldn't be forgotten. In 2004, a new children's camp opened that serves "underprivileged, neglected, at-risk, and abused children between the ages of five to 17," according to the camp's website.[6]

The camp, called the Dare to Dream Camp is free for those kids who cannot afford to pay. Located in Indiana, the camp offers "swimming, paddle boating, canoeing, fishing, arts and crafts, basketball, shuffle board, miniature golf, nature walks, cookouts, bonfires, performing arts, and many other activities that help to life them mentally, physically, emotionally, and spiritually."[7]

The smiles of the kids that will play at the Dare to Dream Camp for years to come is the legacy of Kenny Irwin Jr.

DID YOU KNOW?

The Dare to Dream Camp stands to be a reminder of Kenny Irwin's legacy for years to come. But there's another camp that's doing great things for kids.

The Victory Junction Gang Camp opened in 2004 in North Carolina. The camp honors Adam Petty, who died several months before Kenny on the same New Hampshire track.

The camp is an amazing tribute to Adam. It features colorful buildings designed with a racing theme. There's a pool with fountains to play in, a lake stocked with fish to catch (called "Kiss and Release"), a movie theater, and a beauty shop, among many other neat attractions.

All the children at the camp are suffering from various diseases, and their time away from home or the hospital is supposed to be fun and relaxing. The camp features a full medical staff with state-of-the-art equipment in a building called "The Body Shop." Victory Junction is free for all the kids that attend.

NOTES

Chapter 1

1. *The Associated Press*, "Stewart dedicates win to late rival Irwin." July 9, 2000.

2. Liz Clarke, "NASCAR's Irwin killed in N. Hampshire crash," *The Washington Post*, July 8, 2000.

3. Liz Clarke, "Throttle may have stuck in Irwin's crash," The *Washington Post*, July 9, 2000.

4. Ed Hinton, "NASCAR idles while drivers die," *The Orlando Sentinel*, February 11, 2001. *www. orlandosentinel.com/sports/motorracing/orl-asec-nusafety021101.story?coll=orl-sports-headlines.*

Chapter 5

5. Ryan Smithson, "Irwin Memories: Jr. was gracious at the track," CNNSI.com—Motor Sports, July 7, 2000. *http://sportsillustrated.cnn.com/motorsports/news/2000/07/07/irwin_memories/.*

6. Sponsorship and Contributions—FAQ, "Frequently Asked Questions," Kenny Irwin Jr. Memorial Foundation and Dare to Dream Camp. *www.kennyirwinjrfoundation.org/faq.php.*

7. Ibid.

CHRONOLOGY

1969 Kenneth D. Irwin Jr. born August 5, in Indianapolis, Indiana.

1974 Starts racing quarter midgets and then go-karts.

1985 Starts racing in International Motor Sports Association (IMSA).

1988 Graduates from high school. Works at the family's retail tool shop and races part-time.

1991 Becomes a professional, full-time, midget racer; enters U.S. Auto Club (USAC) National Midget Series.

1993 Is named Rookie of the Year in the USAC Sprint Car Series.

1994 Is named Rookie of the Year in the USAC Silver Crown Sprint Series.

1996 Finishes second in points in the USAC Silver Crown Championship Series; wins the USAC Skoal National Midget Series.

1997 Wins two races, finishes 10th overall for the season, and is named Rookie of the Year in the NASCAR Truck Series. Signs contract with Robert Yates to drive Yates's Ford Taurus No. 28 on the NASCAR Cup Series circuit in the next season.

1998 Wins the most points of any rookie on the Cup circuit and receives the Rookie of the Year trophy. Finishes the season 28th overall, having earned over $1 million through the year.

1999 Finishes third in the first Cup race of the new season, the Daytona 500, and amazes the auto racing world.

2000 Killed on a practice run at Loudon, New Hampshire.

2004 The Kenny Irwin Jr. Foundation's Dare to Dream Camp opens in Indiana.

STATISTICS

NASCAR Craftsman Truck Series

Year	Races	Wins	Top 5	Top 10	Winnings
1996	5	0	1	1	$29,525
1997	26	2	7	10	$302,870
1998	1	0	0	0	$5,625

NASCAR Busch Series

Year	Races	Wins	Top 5	Top 10	Winnings
1999	5	0	2	2	$112,585
2000	9	0	0	2	$62,230

NASCAR (Winston) Cup Series

Year	Races	Wins	Top 5	Top 10	Winnings
1997	4	0	0	1	$61,230
1998	32	0	1	4	$1,433,567
1999	34	0	2	6	$1,995,821
2000	17	0	1	1	$949,436
Career	**87**	**0**	**5**	**12**	**$4,440,054**

FURTHER READING

Bentley, Ross. *Speed Secrets: Professional Race Driving Techniques.* Osceola, WI: Motorbooks International, 1998.

Buckley, James. NASCAR: *Speedway Superstars.* Pleasantville, NY: Readers Digest Children's Publishing, 2004.

Canfield, Jack. *Chicken Soup for the NASCAR Soul.* Deerfield Beach, FL: HCI Publishing, 2003.

Fresina, Michael J., ed. *Thunder and Glory: The 25 Most Memorable Races in NASCAR Winston Cup History.* Worcester, MA: Triumph Books, 2004.

Garrow, Mark. *Dale Earnhardt: The Pass in the Grass and Other Incredible Moments from Racing's Greatest Legend.* Champaign, IL: Sports Publishing, 2001.

Hembree, Mike. *Dale Earnhardt Jr.: Out of the Shadow of Greatness.* Champaign, IL: Sports Publishing, 2003.

McLaurin, Jim. *NASCAR's Most Wanted: The Top 10 Book of Outrageous Drivers, Wild Wrecks, and Other Oddities.* Dulles, VA: Potomac Books, 2001.

Richards, Jon. *Fantastic Cutaway: Speed.* London, UK: Aladdin/Watts, 1997.

Stewart, Mark. *Auto Racing: A History of Cars and Fearless Drivers.* London, UK: Franklin Watts, 1999.

Woods, Bob. *NASCAR: The Greatest Races.* Pleasantville, NY: Reader's Digest, 2004.

BIBLIOGRAPHY

The Associated Press. "Stewart dedicates win to late rival Irwin." July 9, 2000.

Clarke, Liz. "NASCAR's Irwin killed in N. Hampshire crash." *The Washington Post*, July 8, 2000.

———. "Throttle may have stuck in Irwin's crash." The *Washington Post*, July 9, 2000.

Hinton, Ed. "NASCAR idles while drivers die." The *Orlando Sentinel*, February 11, 2001. *www. orlandosentinel.com/sports/motorracing/orl-asec- nusafety021101.story?coll=orl-sports-headlines*.

Sponsorship and Contributions—FAQ. "Frequently Asked Questions." Kenny Irwin Jr. Memorial Foundation and Dare to Dream Camp. *www.kennyirwinjrfoundation. org/faq.php*.

Smithson, Ryan. "Irwin Memories: Jr. was gracious at the track." CNNSI.com—Motor Sports, July 7, 2000. *http://sportsillustrated.cnn.com/motorsports/ news/2000/07/07/irwin_memories/*.

ADDRESSES

The Dare to Dream Camp
75 West County Road, 500S
New Castle, IN 47362

National Association for Stock Car Auto Racing
    (NASCAR)
P.O. Box 2875
Daytona Beach, FL 32120
(386) 253-0611

United States Auto Club (USAC)
National Office
4910 West 16th Street
Speedway, IN 46224
(317) 247-5151

INTERNET SITES

www.nascar.com

> *This site is the best place to start learning more about NASCAR. It has the latest results and driver standings, but there are also pages where readers can learn more about the sport in general. More about Kenny Irwin Jr.'s career can be found here.*

www.jayski.com/teams/42irwin.htm

> *A tribute page to Kenny Irwin Jr.'s life and career. Includes many past links to stories and columns that were written following Kenny's death.*

www.kennyirwinjrfoundation.org

> *The official website for the Dare to Dream Camp, as well as other past links to Kenny Irwin Jr. information. All the information about the camp, including a camper application, can be found on this site.*

NASCAR POINTS SYSTEM

Each NASCAR race winner receives 180 points. The runner-up receives 170. For second through sixth place, the points decrease in 5 point increments. Points awarded drop by four-point increments for drivers in positions seven through 11, and three-point increments up to positions 12 and below. The last place driver, 43rd position, receives 34 points.

Drivers also receive bonuses during the race. Five points for leading a lap and an additional five points for the driver who lead the most laps.

In the Cup series, after the 26th race of the season, any driver within the Top 10 or within 400 points of the leader drive in the "Chase for the Championship." Points are adjusted during "the chase." The leader will begin with 5,050 points and the second place driver starts with 5,045, with each driver receiving five points lower depending on their year's Cup series standings.

Drivers are not the only ones in a points race. Owners also have a points system. Unlike drivers, however, owners can earn points by just entering a race. If an owner has a pair of drivers and one fails to qualify, the owner still receives points for the non-qualifying effort. On race day, the fastest non-qualifier receives 31 points, which is three points lower than 43rd position. The scale continues to decline, the lowest possible amount being awarded being one point.

Even car manufacturers have their own points race. The company whose car wins first, earns nine points. Second place receives six points, third place earns four points and fourth place earns three points.

NASCAR SIGNAL FLAGS

BLACK: Come into the pits immediately for consultation. This in combination with a red flag means the end of a practice session.

BLACK WITH WHITE CROSS: A car will no longer be scored until the car shown the previous black flag stops in the pits for a consultation.

BLUE WITH YELLOW STRIPE: A faster car is approaching behind, so watch in mirrors. This flag is not a mandatory signal for slower cars to move to the side to let faster cars pass.

CHECKERED: Race complete.

GREEN: The race has begun. This flag also signals when the track is clear and cars may proceed at speed.

RED: Unsafe track conditions. Cars must stop at a designated location. This flag usually means bad weather conditions, medical emergencies, or a blocked track.

WHITE: One lap remaining.

YELLOW (CAUTION): Slow down, hold your position behind the pace car. This flag means that the track is not clear, usually from an accident, debris, weather, or mechanical failure. NASCAR rules let cars bunch up behind the pace car. Lead-lap car start in the outside lane while lapped cars begin to the inside.

YELLOW WITH RED VERTICAL STRIPES: Slippery conditions or debris on track ahead.

www.nascar.com/2002/kyn/nascar_101/12/03/flags/index. html

NASCAR SAFETY

In order to protect the drivers of a race car, NASCAR requires certain safety precautions in the car's design and the driver's attire.

A head-and-neck—A restraint on either side of the head and neck, keeps the driver's head secure.

Fire-retardant suit—Made from Proban or Nomax, which are thick fire-resistant materials. Drivers wear special shoes made from these materials as well to protect from foot burns from the hot car temperatures, a common injury while driving.

Helmet—Contains an outer layer made with Kevlar and two inner layers to help protect and cushion a driver's head.

Harness—Made from thick, padded nylon webbing, NASCAR harnesses have five straps: two coming down from the shoulders, two across the driver's waist, and one up between the legs. The harness does not stretch like a street car belt. NASCAR harnesses secure the driver to the seat, so in case of a wreck, the driver is not jolted.

Nets—Covering the driver's window to keep debris out and a driver's arms from flailing out during a crash or roll-over.

Roll cage—Sturdy safety framework built inside the car to help the car maintain its shape if it rolls or is hit.

Seats—Seats are bolted in several places to the roll cage so the seat will not be thrown from the car. Seats also wrap around the driver's ribcage, and often shoulders, to distribute force across body, instead of on a small section of the torso.

Windshields—Made from Lexon, debris will not shatter the windshield. The soft, but sturdy matter will deflect or scratch instead of shatter.

NASCAR TRACKS

Atlanta Motor Speedway	Hampton, GA
Autodromo Hermanos Rodriguez	Mexico City, Mexico
Bristol Motor Speedway	Bristol, TN
California Speedway	Fontana, CA
Chicagoland Speedway	Joliet, IL
Darlington Raceway	Darlington, SC
Daytona Int'l Speedway	Daytona Beach, FL
Dover Int'l Speedway	Dover, DE
Gateway Int'l Raceway	Madison, IL
Homestead-Miami Speedway	Homestead, FL
Indianapolis Motor Speedway	Speedway, IN
Indianapolis Raceway Park	Indianapolis, IN
Infineon Raceway	Sonoma, CA
Kansas Speedway	Kansas City, KS
Kentucky Speedway	Sparta, KY
Las Vegas Motor Speedway	Las Vegas, NV
Lowe's Motor Speedway	Concord, NC
Mansfield Motorsports Speedway	Mansfield, Ohio
Martinsville Speedway	Martinsville, VA
Memphis Motorsports Park	Memphis, TN
Michigan Int'l Speedway	Brooklyn, MI
The Milwaukee Mile	West Allis, WI
Nashville Superspeedway	Lebanon, TN
Nazareth Speedway	Nazareth, PA

New Hampshire Int'l Speedway	Loudon, NH
Phoenix Int'l Raceway	Avondale, AZ
Pikes Peak Int'l Raceway	Fountain, CO
Pocono Raceway	Long Pond, PA
Richmond Int'l Raceway	Richmond, VA
Talladega Superspeedway	Talladega, AL
Texas Motor Speedway	Fort Worth, TX
Watkins Glen International	Watkins Glen International, NY

Photo Credits:

© AP/Wide World Photos: Cover, 7, 8, 12, 14, 20, 23, 28, 31, 37, 39, 41, 45, 46; © Getty Images: 9, 18, 25, 26, 34.

INDEX

ABOUT THE AUTHORS

Ann Graham Gaines received her graduate degrees in American Civilization and Library and Information Science from the University of Texas at Austin. Specializing in biographies and nonfiction, Gaines has been a freelance writer for 21 years. She lives by Gonzalez, Texas with her husband and their four children.

Jeff Gluck covers NASCAR, high school sports and the Atlantic Coast Conference for the *Rocky Mount Telegram* in North Carolina. A University of Delaware graduate, Gluck has also lived in California, Minnesota, and Colorado, visiting a total of 45 states along the way. Gluck has covered the Super Bowl, the Daytona 500, a Duke-North Carolina men's college basketball game, and has attended three NCAA Final Fours.

Local coverage includes every high school sport from football to swimming, as well as the Double-A Carolina Mudcats baseball team, and NCAA Division III N.C. Wesleyan College.

Gluck and his wife, Jaime, reside in Rocky Mount, North Carolina.